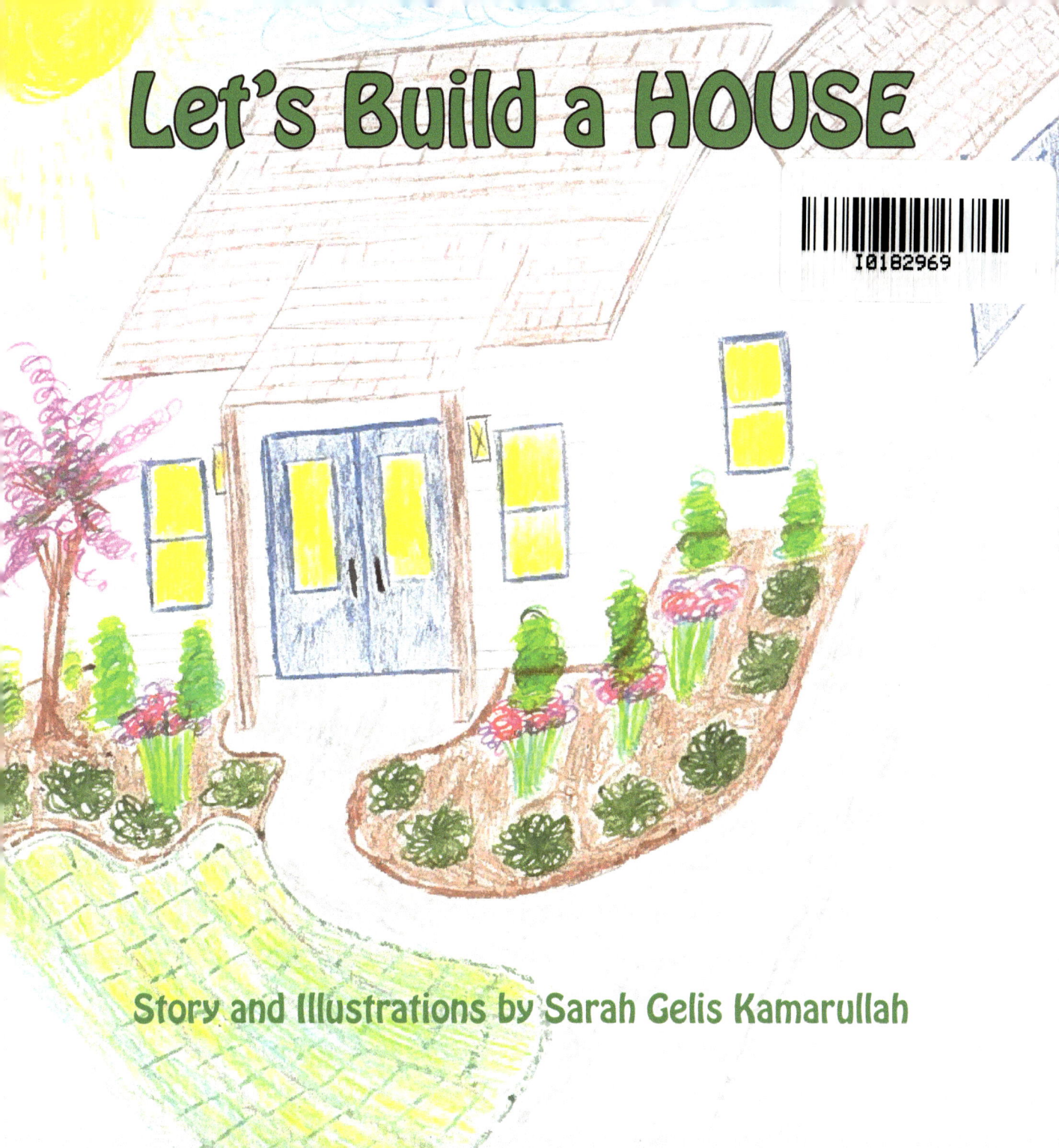

Let's Build a HOUSE

Story and Illustrations by Sarah Gelis Kamarullah

Let's Build a House
Copyright © 2024—Sarah Gelis Kamarullah
ALL RIGHTS RESERVED UNDER U.S., PAN-AMERICAN AND INTERNATIONAL COPYRIGHTS. No part of this publication may be reproduced, stored in a retrieval system or transmitted in any form by mechanical, electronic, photocopying, recording or otherwise without the prior written consent of the author.

Bible references marked ESV are from the *The Holy Bible, English Standard Version*, copyright © 2001 by Crossway Bibles, a publishing ministry of Good News Publishers. References marked NIV are from *The Holy Bible, New International Version*, copyright © 1973, 1978, 1984, 2011 by Biblica, Colorado Springs, Colorado. References marked WEB are from the World English Bible®, public domain. References marked NASB are from the *New American Standard Bible*, copyright © 1960, 1962, 1963, 1968, 1971, 1972, 1973, 1975, 1977 by the Lockman Foundation, La Habra, California. References marked NKJV are from *The Holy Bible, New King James Version*, copyright © 1979, 1980, 1982, by Thomas Nelson, Inc., Nashville, Tennessee. All rights reserved. Used by permission. Words in all caps are the author's emphasis.

Published by:

Little Oaks Publishing
www.thepublishedword.com

ISBN: 978-1-964665-12-2

Printed on demand in the U.S., the U.K. and Australia
For Worldwide Distribution

Let's Build a HOUSE

This easy read not only lays out the steps to building a house; it also shows foundational truths about God and His love for His children. It is filled with wonderful scriptures to speak over your little one, no matter how big or small they might be.

Little Oaks

ISBN 978-1-964665-12-2

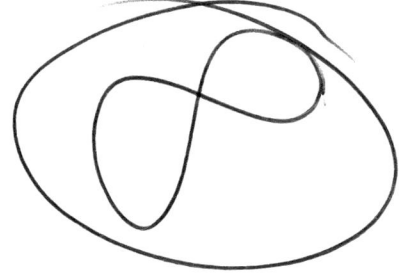

To my precious GK and TK
With all the love in my heart -SK

Make me to know your ways, O Lord;

teach me your paths.

Lead me in your truth and teach me,

for you are the God of my salvation;

for you I wait all the day long.

Psalm 25:4-5, ESV

When building a house, we must first start with a firm foundation. Let's find out what God's Word says about Jesus becoming our Foundation.

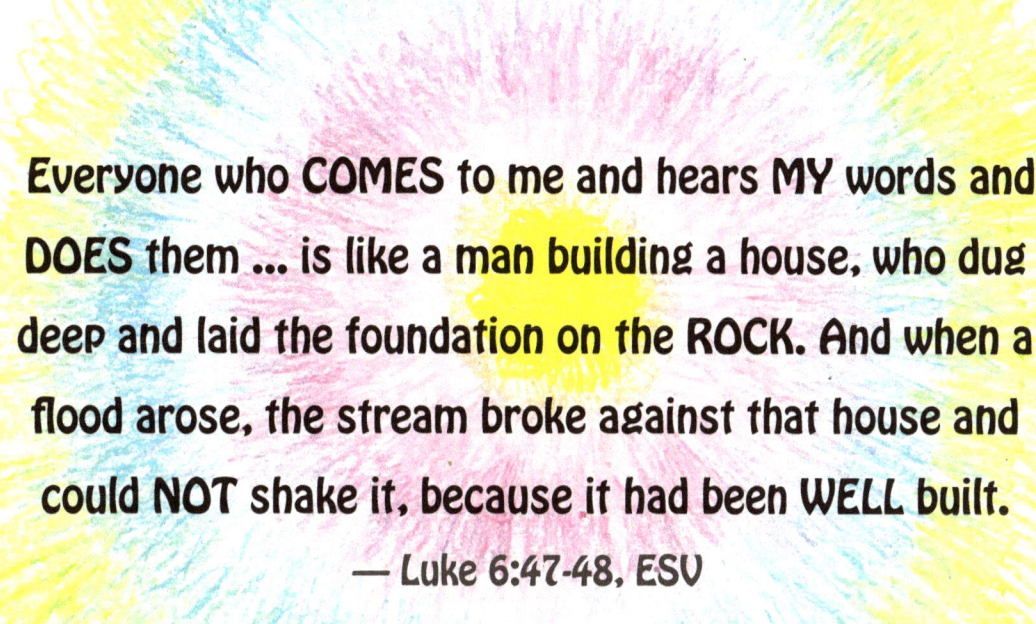

Everyone who **COMES** to me and hears **MY** words and **DOES** them ... is like a man building a house, who dug deep and laid the foundation on the **ROCK**. And when a flood arose, the stream broke against that house and could **NOT** shake it, because it had been **WELL** built.

— Luke 6:47-48, ESV

Next, let's start the framework. We need something strong that we can trust.

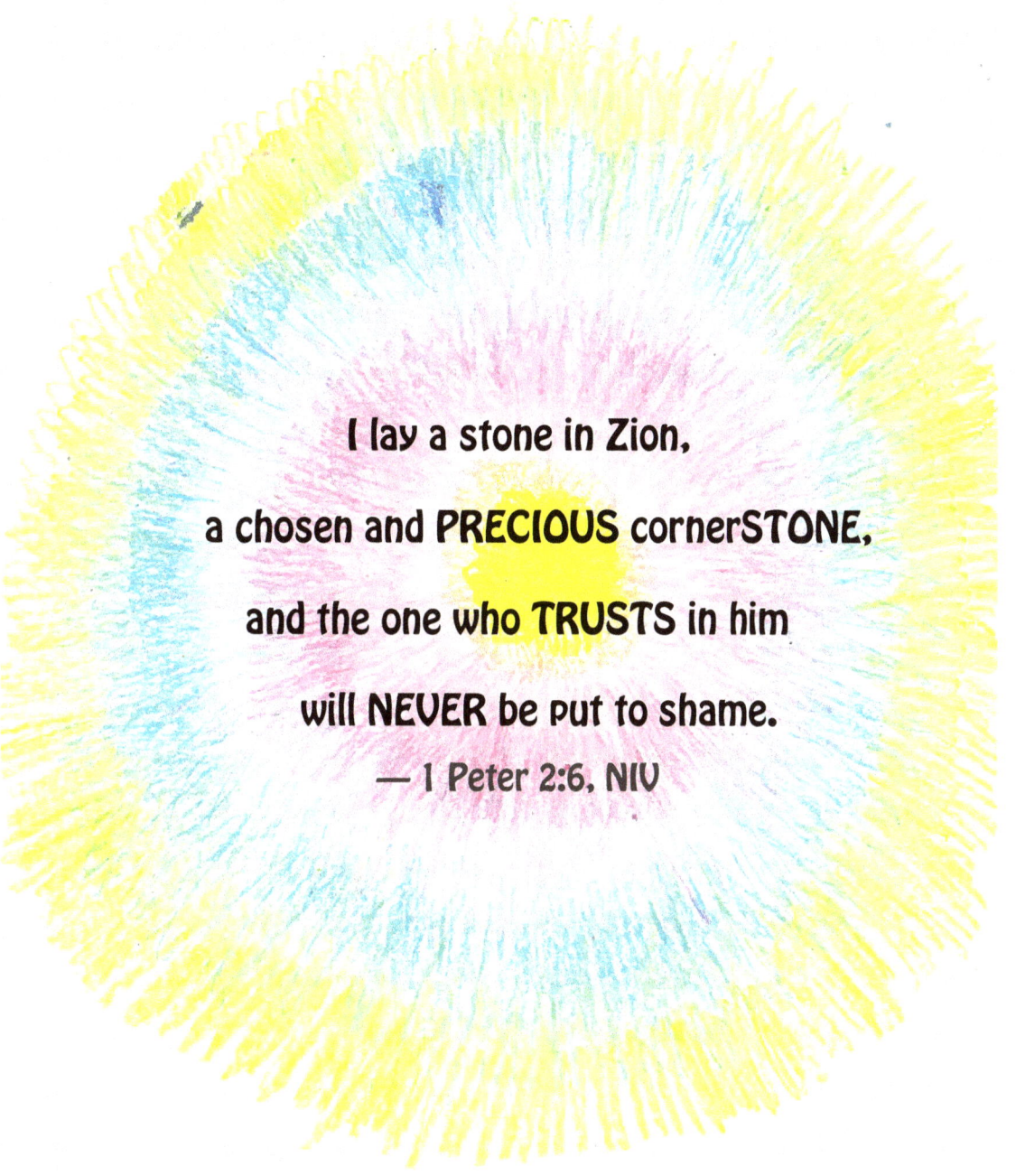

Now we are ready to put on the roof for shelter.

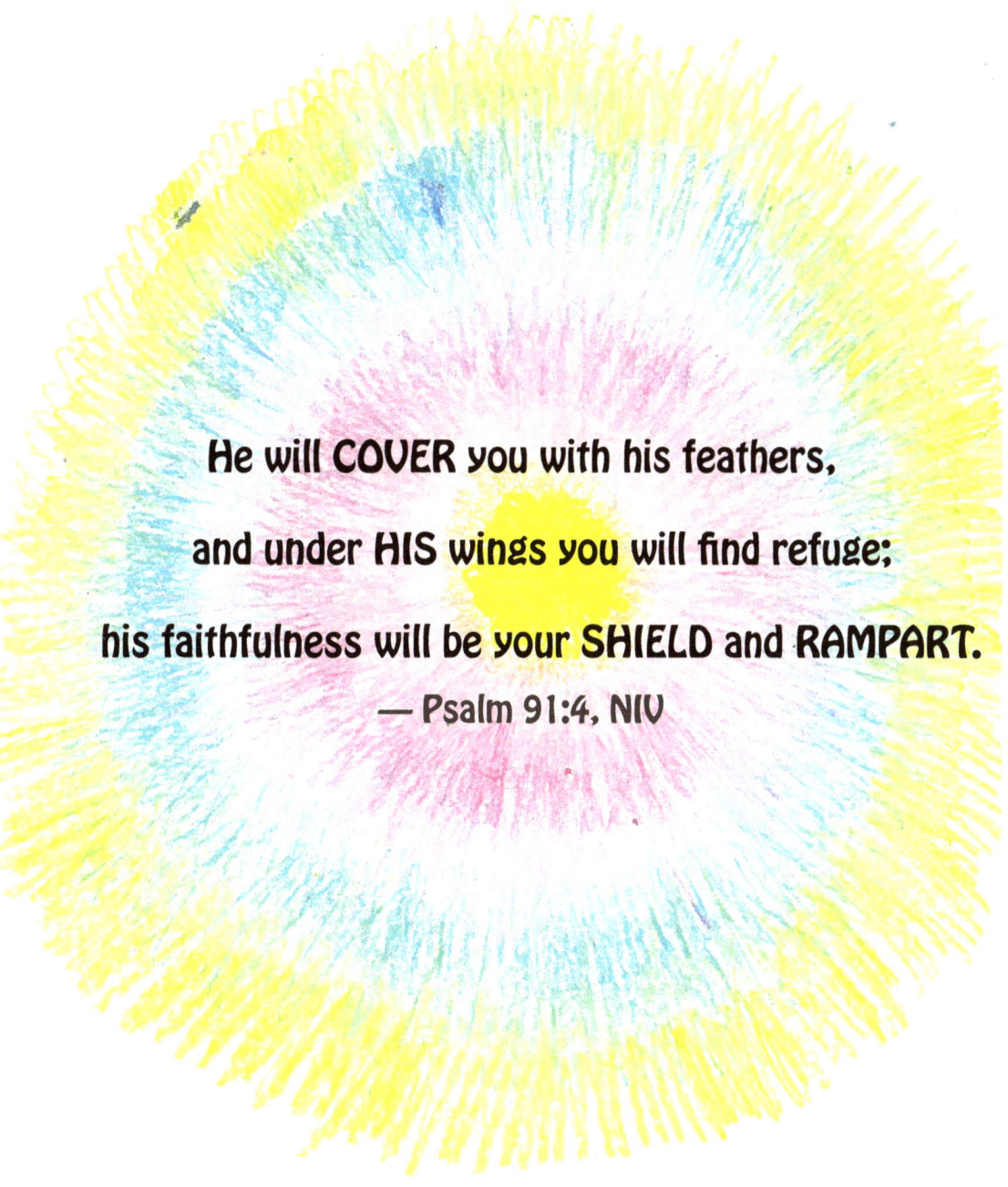

Next, we will install doors and windows.

It's a good thing we installed the doors and windows. Did you see that storm brewing? But don't worry, here is what Jesus says about storms.

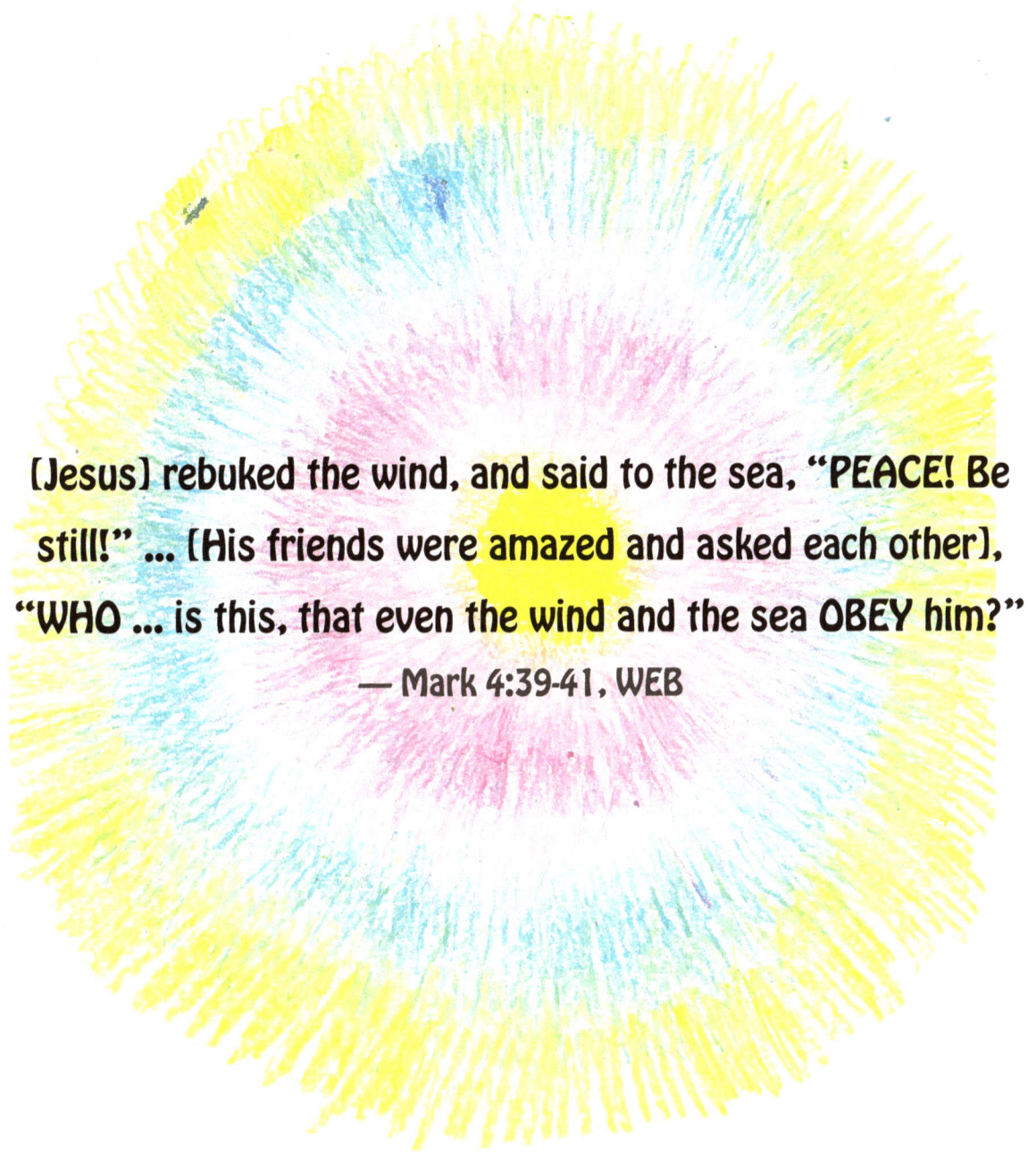

Installing sturdy siding on our house will keep us protected.

We can't forget about the need for lights.

Last, but not least, let's plant a flower bed that will dress up the house nicely.